Dear Nancy.

You are always so
Cheerful and Spreading
hope. Keep hope alive!

02/08/2024

# THE
# VOICE
## OF
# HOPE

SEVEN STORIES FROM A CHAPLAIN ON
HEARING HOPE IN THE DARKEST HOUR

CHAPLAIN DESMOND HAYE,
MPH, MDIV., BCC

WESTBOW
PRESS®
A DIVISION OF THOMAS NELSON
& ZONDERVAN

WestBow Press books may be ordered through booksellers or by contacting:

WestBow Press
A Division of Thomas Nelson & Zondervan
1663 Liberty Drive
Bloomington, IN 47403
www.westbowpress.com
844-714-3454

Interior Image Credit: cheriefox.com

ISBN: 978-1-6642-8956-7 (sc)
ISBN: 978-1-6642-8955-0 (e)

Library of Congress Control Number: 2023901018

Print information available on the last page.

WestBow Press rev. date:   01/27/2023

This book is dedicated to my wife,
Stacey Ann; my son, Caleb; my mother,
Madge Haye; and the many healthcare
professionals, patients, and families
I have journeyed with over the years

# CONTENTS

# FOREWORD

*Hope is seeing that there is light
despite all of the darkness.*
Desmond Tutu

OUR COUNTRY AND THE HEALTHCARE INDUSTRY
saw a season of darkness through the global pandemic.
Physical illness was not only all around, but also
mental illness caused by fear and isolation. We were
not unfamiliar with death and dying, but we were
unfamiliar with the amount and speed at which it was
happening. Through dark times like this, the quote
from Desmond Tutu rings even more true because
we were in such dire need of light. Positive light that
could revive weary spirits. Positive light that could
heal mental and emotional wounds. Positive light that
would remind us of whom we serve and how He has
overcome the world.

I am so thrilled that my friend and colleague, Desmond Haye, took the time to write about the powerful subject of hope. As you read this book, I pray that you will be inspired to embrace hope and find ways to bring hope to the world. Wouldn't it be powerful if we all found ways to turn on a light for our fellow man?

Kenneth Rose
CEO, Texas Health Hospital Mansfield

# INTRODUCTION

Wʜᴀᴛ ɪꜰ ʜᴏᴘᴇ ᴄᴏᴜʟᴅ ꜱᴘᴇᴀᴋ ᴛᴏ ʏᴏᴜ? Wʜᴀᴛ ᴡᴏᴜʟᴅ it say? How would it sound in your ears?

How would hope sound to a husband and wife who experience the death of a baby?

What would hope say to a professional who has heard the unexpected prognosis of end-stage cancer?

How would hope sound in the ear of a single mother being evicted for the thirteenth time?

Perhaps you have been upended by the pandemic or are journeying through the dark night of the soul, and you are wondering what's next. The book The Voice of Hope will inspire you to hold on to hope no matter the circumstances. As a chaplain, your ministry may be somewhat ecumenical but primarily founded on the Bible. As a hospice chaplain, you deal with people-both care recipients and later their bereaved loved ones-at what is ordinarily the most bleakly hopeless time of life. In these dark moments, inspiring hope is so crucial, and this is the aim of this book.

Each chapter in *The Voice of Hope* begins with an exemplary story and concludes with a short recitative prayer that the reader (addressed as 'you') may use to meditate on the teaching, followed by a set of questions to think and talk through.

We hope this little compendium will find its way into homes, healthcare institutions, and more so, into the hearts of individuals across the globe.

# 1

## Hope Says You Are Not Alone

As the chaplain sat at the bedside of a dying care recipient diagnosed with a terminal illness and given days to live, the woman asked, "Chaplain, what's next?"

The loaded question ran like electricity through the chaplain's body and caused him to confront his own mortality. As she talked about her accomplishments and the many places she had been, she turned toward the chaplain and said, "All this pales in the presence of my troubling question."

The chaplain nodded in agreement and held her hand as the tears washed her shriveled face. The chaplain's internal thoughts were many, but there was no quick fix for this one. As he listened empathically to her and celebrated her lived experiences, the words "You are not alone" came from his lips.

She heard the chaplain, squeezed his hands, and replied, "I am glad to know you have been called to walk this dark path with me."

Weeks passed, and one morning several visits later, she died holding the chaplain's hands as he visited her home. Her last words were, "Chaplain, I am glad our paths have crossed, and you did not try to fix me but held my hands as we journeyed through this dark night of the soul."

Reflecting on that experience, the chaplain was assured that she found peace. She died with the sound of hope when he said, "You are not alone." She confided in the chaplain that while she could not fully comprehend what would happen next, she was content she was at a place where hope whispers, and she was not alone.

If hope can speak, its voice might be heard to say, "You are not alone. You, who have been maligned, mistreated, and afflicted, are not alone. You, who have endured the agony of giving birth and watching your precious child die, are not alone. You, whose strong body has been emaciated by a dreadful disease for which there is no cure, are not alone. You, whose body was thrown from that vehicle, who lives with the scars, are not alone. You, who must walk the difficult pathway of grief and loss, are not alone."

Hope reminds us we are not alone, for death cannot steal the courage of one who knows there is something beyond. Paul, the Christian apostle and theologian, wrote:

> Behold, I show you a mystery: We shall not all sleep; but we shall all be changed in a moment, in the twinkling of an eye, at the last trumpet. The trumpet shall sound, the dead shall be raised incorruptible, and we shall be changed. For this corruptible must put on incorruption, and this mortal must put on immortality. (1 Corinthians 15:51-53, KJ21)

Hope says there is a brighter tomorrow beyond the darkness of the tomb. Hope says when you walk through the dark valley of scary diagnosis and painful prognosis, God is with you, and you will never walk alone. Amid pain and perplexing circumstances,

3

hope speaks words of assurance and comfort. Hope says death will one day die, but those who trust in God will live again.

## Your Meditation Moment

Today, I hold on to hope—the hope that whispers in my pain, grief, loss, and anxieties that I am not alone. Teach me to hold fast to the promise that death cannot steal the courage of one who knows there is more beyond. Amen.

## Think and Talk It Through

1. Reflect on a time when you felt alone. What brought you comfort?
2. What can you share with someone who might feel hopeless and alone?
3. Connect with three individuals who live alone, and share a word of hope with them.

# 2

## Hope Says You
## Are Loved

THE HALLS OF THE NEW HOSPITAL WERE BUZZING with activity, but her sobbing and shrieking cries could be heard above the monitors, call bells, and ringing telephones. It was a cry of desperation. It was a cry you could not escape, no matter how hard you tried.

As the chaplain walked toward her room after being called to sit with her, he was nervous, apprehensive, thinking about the nonstop cry. When he entered her room, she seemed to weep even louder. She was lying on the bed, presenting as a middle-aged woman with a thin, frail body twisted in the hospital sheets. Her face was wet with tears. Her eyes were wild with sadness. Her hair was unkempt. Her pain was palpable. Her room was bare, and a small knapsack was sitting on the chair next to her. "He does not love me anymore," she said.

The chaplain was speechless. What could he say to this woman to bring comfort? Should he speak? Should he be quiet? How long would this last? The chaplain's inadequacies became evident as these questions raced through his mind. He struggled with the internal dialogue but leaned in with courage. "I am sorry to hear he does not love you anymore." And from that moment, an awkward silence swept over the room.

The chaplain sat there silently. As he observed her, the pupils in her eyes dilated, and she closed her eyelids as if she was in total shock. A deafening silence ensued, and the chaplain held the space, wondering. He wondered about who she was. Where had she come from? Who did not love her? What was so important about that love? How did she get here? Was this the only source of her distress? He was curious about her past, her family, and her faith or lack thereof. But the silence did not end. Now that her cries had abated, the chaplain could see, in his peripheral vision, nurses passing by the room with a look of curious concern. Something mysterious had happened, and they wanted to be sure everybody was okay.

As the chaplain remained still and resisted the urge to ask questions, the woman spoke through her tears. "I did not know what love should look, sound, or feel like until I met him." What continued was a deeply personal and emotionally moving encounter between this woman and the chaplain. She shared her life of rejection, pain, resentment, lack of love, and suffering, and how that life changed when she met her partner. Now she felt betrayed and forsaken, and the pain was unbearable. Her psychological state was affected profoundly, and her cry arose from disbelief that the one who taught her about love could turn his back on her.

As they processed the emotional and spiritual pain, the chaplain watched as her body, which had been so tense, relaxed. Her tears dwindled. She opened her eyes and looked at him intently. "Can I ever be loved again?"

The chaplain listened reflectively, then invited her to contemplate a pure, holy, and kind love that would not leave her. She said, "I want that love." They explored what that love might look like for her, and she became excited about its prospects.

In the chaplain's encounters with her, he saw renewed hope. He saw a broken soul being mended by a love stronger than death. Paul's admonition to the Corinthian church gave her a deep sense of relief from the perplexing pain of the past. The chaplain would never forget the day he read these words to her:

> Though I speak with the tongues of men and of angels, but have not love, I have become sounding brass or a clanging cymbal. And though I have *the gift of* prophecy, and understand all mysteries and all knowledge, and though I have all faith, so that I could remove mountains, but have not to love, I am nothing. And though I bestow all my goods to feed *the poor,* and though I give my body to be burned, but have not love, it profits me nothing. Love suffers long *and* is kind; love does not envy; love does not parade itself, is not puffed up; does not behave rudely, does not seek its own, is not provoked,

thinks no evil; does not rejoice in
iniquity, but rejoices in the truth;
bears all things, believes all things,
hopes all things, endures all things …
And now abide faith, hope, love, these
three; but the greatest of these *is* love.
(1 Corinthians 13:1-4,13, NKJV)

She became tearful, and the chaplain invited her
to embrace the reality of her loss and receive love
stronger than hate.

So often in life, people live with the pain of
rejection, hoping that their love cups will be filled
by someone else. They walk around yearning for the
affirmation of others when hope says you are already
loved. Yes, you are loved by God, the essence of
love. You are loved with a kind love, not an envious,
boastful, or rude love. You are loved when you have
faced rejection by those you trusted. You are loved
even in your pain. You are loved more than you
ever imagined, and a recognition of this love is the
beginning of healing, health, and happiness.

When hope speaks, it reminds us that our broken
and bewildered past fades in the surpassing love
of the Divine. When hope speaks, it whispers of a

love that can transform hard hearts, elevate troubled minds, reconcile broken relationships, and tear down caste, creed, and religious bigotry. To the man in the shanty town, hope says, "You are loved." To the angry child within crying out for the father who was never present, hope says, "You are loved." To the surgeon in the operating room, whose heart is torn by an unstable home but who must accomplish one more surgery, hope says, "You are loved." To the nurse at the bedside who watches another person breathe their last breath and must grapple with their own mortality, hope says, "You are loved." Even to CEOs, CFOs, and leaders who must find answers to life's challenges, hope says, "You are loved, and love wins every time."

To every person who has ever felt the pain of rejection, betrayal, and hate, you are loved. May hope rise in your heart with a song whose rhythm will beat within, saying you are loved and loveable, as a loving reminder that light will ever be more potent than darkness.

## Your Meditation Moment

Remind me today that hope says I am loved. Pour into my empty heart the beauty, kindness, and tender compassion of that love which is stronger than death. Amen.

## Think and Talk It Through

1. Think of at least three persons who genuinely love you.
2. How have you experienced the love of the Divine on your journey?
3. When was the last time you expressed your love to a family member or close friend?

# 3

## Hope Says You Can Find Peace

IT WAS HIS SEVENTH VISIT AS THE HOSPICE chaplain to this home. The previous encounters were challenging. The disease had made inroads, and it appeared that the inevitable would happen next.

The care recipient was alert, awake, and oriented, but with a flat affect. He had experienced so many losses over the last several weeks. He had lost his individuality. He was now in total care and struggled with the rapid changes. He was still mourning the loss of his beloved wife and confidante of fifty years, and no language could describe the depths of his pain. He was mourning the loss also of his relationship with his daughter, who had not spoken to him for more than five years. He was conflicted, bitter, hurt, angry, and without peace.

During the chaplain's visits, they made baby steps. He enjoyed and valued the chaplain's nonjudgmental, anxiety-free presence. He soon discovered that he could be angry, frustrated, and happy around the chaplain, all during the same visit. The chaplain often wondered whether he was making a difference, but the care recipient had taught the chaplain many things during those seven visits. He taught the chaplain the value of patience and allowing the care recipient to lead in the visits. He taught chaplain that he did not have the answers to the troubling questions of life, and that's okay. The chaplain has had many *aha* moments in these visits as he learned how to sit with pain and remain present for those who must journey this pathway.

The care recipient expressed that he had made peace with everything and everyone—except his daughter, with whom he had not spoken for five years. The chaplain and the team had worked hard at trying to find and connect him with his daughter but remained unsuccessful. Finally, one day, as the chaplain was about to leave, the care recipient said, "Chaplain, it's okay; I am at peace." His expression was hard to comprehend, for his source of distress was the irreconcilable differences between him and his daughter.

However, the chaplain had learned that peace is not the absence of struggles but the presence of the Divine. Sometimes we do not have the answer, and it is okay. For peace is not some ethereal experience but a calm resolve that you will be all right after doing your best. Finding peace in the dark chapters of our lives can help bring closure. The peace of God will enfold hurting hearts and release contentment to troubled souls. No wonder Jesus, the great peace speaker, says, "Peace, I leave you, my peace I give you; not as the world gives, do I give to you. Do not let your hearts be troubled, nor fearful" (John 14:27, KJV).

Hope says you can find peace in the storms of life. Hope says peace does not negate trials but encourages confidence in the One who is bigger than our fears. Hope whispers to those devastated by hurricanes, tsunamis, earthquakes, and school shootings that while our world is imperfect, we can experience rest in our quiet places. Hope speaks peace to those in war-torn countries who must bury their dead, pick up the pieces, and move on. Hope says you can find peace when you have lost your family at the hands of a dreadful virus. Finally, hope says you can find peace when you feel alone.

The peace that hope speaks of is personal. We can experience serenity and calm within our souls no matter the turbulence outside us. You can experience this sweet peace which can transform you so that external forces cannot steal it. The peace that hope speaks of is promising. As hope speaks peace, it shares a peace that promises to heal sorrowful souls and give a calm resolve in the tragedies of life.

## Your Meditation Moment

Prince of Peace, speak into my soul today the calm assurance that I can find harmony in You amid life's storms. Amen.

## Think and Talk It Through

1. What brings you peace in life's challenging moments?

2. How can you foster an atmosphere of peace in your daily life?

3. Is there someone or something you need to make peace with today?

# 4

## Hope Says You
## Have Joy

THE ROOM WAS FILLED WITH A DEEP SENSE OF JOY. Family members were together in the hospital room to share this happy moment. There is no greater joy for a family than adding a newborn. The faces of those surrounding the bed expressed this joy as they all looked lovingly at the newborn in her mother's arms. The look on the new mom's face showed her excitement mixed with tiredness. She had labored long, and now the pain was eclipsed by a joy no words could describe. These joyful moments are reminders that all is not lost in our world. Amid the pain of searing loss, we find beautiful reminders that reveal our world is still a wonderful place.

When hope speaks, it whispers of a joy this world cannot give or take away. As the chaplain gazed upon that newborn in her mom's loving arms, hope whispered, "They have joy." Life will not always be filled with challenging days and lonely nights, for joy will not leave us alone. Hope says joy is a positive emotion distinct from gratitude or contentment. Hope says joy is internal and is not swayed by external factors. Hope says a mind transformed by the Divine causes joy. Hope says joy will affect our happiness over time and inspire us to live a whole life.

In life's journey, be assured that you can have joy. No one can steal this deep-abiding feeling from you, for even nature exudes joy in the power of the Divine. The writer of Chronicles reminds us:

> Let the sea roar, and all that fills it;
> let the field exult, and everything in it!
> Then shall the trees of the forest sing
> for joy
> before the Lord, for he comes to judge
> the earth.

> Oh give thanks to the Lord, for he is
> good;
> for his steadfast love endures forever!
> (1 Chronicles 16:32-34, ESV)

So when you face the turbulence of life, be assured of soul-saving joy. When a lingering illness is your constant companion, hope says you can find joy in the presence of the Divine. When you walk through life's valleys, and it seems dark and lonely, hope says joy will attend you. When you cradle a newborn and imagine the prospects of a bright future, hope says joy will accompany you: "For I reckon that the sufferings of this present time are not worthy to be compared with the glory which shall be revealed in us" (Romans 8:18, KJV).

## Your Meditation Moment

Today, I choose joy. I prefer to experience the soul-saving joy of knowing there is hope. I crave Your presence, so my joy will always be complete. I anticipate the eternal happiness of Your company in the sweet forever. Amen.

## Think and Talk It Through

1. Reflect on a moment in your life when you experienced absolute joy. What was it like for you, and what lessons can you draw from that experience?

2. What are some things you can do to maintain a joyful attitude?

3. What are some hindrances to joy in your life?

# 5

## Hope Says You Will Triumph over Tragedy

It was shaping up to be a quiet Saturday night in the hospital. The chaplain walked the floors and greeted the teams as they provided compassionate care on the night shift. When the code came across the intercom system, the chaplain had just returned to his desk when he felt the beeper pulsating on his hip. He rushed to the emergency room, and the scene was chaotic. Several patients were dead, and others were covered with blood. Doctors, nurses, radiologists, and technicians were frantically triaging and managing the situation. It was a fatal four-vehicle collision, and several young men were affected.

As the ER became busier, family members arrived and sought answers regarding their loved ones. The chaplain ushered the families to the large consultation room for greater control and to de-escalate the horrible crisis. As he surveyed the room, he saw faces filled with shock and fear, and the tears were flowing profusely.

The chaplain introduced himself. He could feel the deep sadness in the room. "A terrible tragedy has occurred tonight, and we are all confused," he said. "I am sorry, but we will journey together and try to make sense of what has happened."

Across the room, a young man screamed, "Why?" Sensing the immensity of grief in the room and the reality that no explanation would suffice, the chaplain remained silent. The moment called for silence. The silence spoke eloquently to each person in the room. The silence allowed each person to contemplate and experience whatever emotion they were experiencing.

As they sat quietly, the ER physician came in to give an update on the status of each care recipient. It was a profoundly emotional experience as he broke the news to parents who had lost an only child and wives who had lost their husbands. The expressions

24

of emotions varied from person to person, but all felt the common thread of human pain.

Tragedies are inevitable. The circumstances of life sometimes offer painful experiences that pierce our hearts. The sudden loss of a loved one, a tragic accident taking several young lives, and the premature death of a young child are but a few of life's painful tragedies. The tragedies of life remind us of human frailty. But even amid all these horrific experiences, hope whispers that you will triumph over tragedy.

When hope speaks in the tragic circumstances of life, it reminds grief-stricken individuals of their frailty. We are frail, and tragedies are inevitable, but hope is more persistent each time. Hope looks beyond the tragic circumstances of this life to a time when we will all triumph over our pain. Tragedy says, "I will take your loved one from you," but hope says, "The grave is not final." Tragedy says, "I will change the trajectory of your future." Still, hope says, "I will transform your test into a testimony."

Triumphing over tragedy will call upon you to change your perspective, but it is always for the better. In the most challenging moments of life, we receive God's greatest blessing as a reward for the crucibles we have been through. Life can be daunting, but hope speaks of victory over our adversities. You are a victor. You are a winner, for the one who gains triumph over tragedy understands the personification of hope. No wonder the apostle Peters exhorts:

> Beloved, think it not strange concerning the fiery trial which is to try you, as though some strange thing happened unto you: But rejoice, inasmuch as ye are partakers of Christ's sufferings; that, when his glory shall be revealed, ye may be glad also with exceeding joy. (1 Peter 4:12-13, KJV)

Hope whispers amid life's strange and foreboding tragedies that you can triumph over your pain and fear.

## Your Meditation Moment

Dear God, help me to know that the tragic circumstances of life cannot separate me from your love. Walk with me through the dark valley of my many questions to a place of triumph. Amen.

## Think and Talk It Through

1. Reflect on a tragic life experience and the lessons you learned from it.
2. What brings you great comfort in your time of tragedy?
3. Reflect on how you can support others in times of tragedy.

# 6

## Hope Says Suffering Will Not Last

The chaplain was serving in New York City at the height of the COVID-19 pandemic. His experience in that city at a time of such great suffering will be etched forever in his mind. The chaplain witnessed the many deaths, fears, and uncertainties among healthcare workers. His ministry took on new meaning during this time of immense suffering and pain. He was called to journey in new ways with the families on hospice. Yet the disenfranchised grief was real. Families could not mourn the loss of their loved ones in ways that would encourage closure and reconciliation with grief. Funeral services were reduced to a ten-minute committal service in a cemetery. Mourning in culturally appropriate ways seemed stifled.

Once, the chaplain was standing in a cemetery doing committals. A long line of cars with mourners was slowly moving through designated areas where their loved ones were lying in caskets, ready to be interred. He could see the agony of unresolved grief across their faces. He could feel their pain. The tears of the brokenhearted were not wiped away, nor were their souls comforted. The chaplain's heart went out in compassion. Still, due to social distancing and other regulations, it was challenging to journey with these broken families. The immensity of human suffering became his daily contemplation.

He wondered much about suffering and when it would end. The chaplain wrestled with many questions, but hope always whispered that suffering will not last. Human grief will not last, for it shall be eclipsed by everlasting love, joy, and peace. Over the last couple of years, we have suffered so much globally. We have been plunged into lives of social isolation, but hope says we shall rise from the ashes. Hope speaks in clear tones that suffering will not last. The suffering of this life shall be eclipsed by a peace that the world cannot give or take away. Jesus was true when he said, "Peace I leave with you; my peace I give you. I do not give to you as the world gives. Do not let your hearts be troubled and do not be afraid" (John 14:27, KJV).

Hope cries out to humanity languishing in unimaginable suffering and says that it will not last. Hope says our suffering will not escape the eyes of the Divine: "for the eyes of the Lord run to and fro throughout the whole earth, to give strong support to those whose heart is blameless toward him" (2 Chronicles 16:9, ESV). God is with us in our suffering; we are not alone. God will help us in our suffering, for His strong support will be a fortress of help in our time of distress.

Those who suffer can rest in the hope found in the promises of scripture. So the God of hope speaks to us, saying, "Surely I am with you always, to the very end of the age" (Matthew 28:2, NIV).

> When you pass through the waters,
> I will be with you;
> and when you pass through the rivers,
> they will not sweep over you.

When you walk through the fire,
you will not be burned;
the flames will not set you ablaze.
(Isaiah 43:2, NIV)

"For I know the plans I have for you,"
declares the Lord, "plans to prosper
you and not to harm you, plans to
give you hope and a future." (Jeremiah
29:11 NIV)

These promises are timely reminders that suffering will not last. We shall, amid our suffering, turn to the God who speaks hope.

## Your Meditation Moment

As I walk through the dark vale of suffering, I fear no pain, for you are with me. Help me to know that suffering will not last. Amen.

## Think and Talk It Through

1. Reflect on a time of deep suffering. What kept you going?

2. What can you do to help those who are suffering around you?

3. Do you think suffering is a necessary part of the human experience? Explain your perspective.

# 7

## Hope Says There Is a Brighter Tomorrow

THE CHAPLAIN'S THOUGHTS WERE RUNNING A MILE a minute as he sat on the platform waiting to share the eulogy for a care recipient who had passed the week before. How could he be a comforting presence in this situation? The chaplain had met the deceased during a grave crisis after he lost his son and his wife of more than fifty years. They developed a tremendous relationship. He told the chaplain stories about the war, faith, courage, and his view on tomorrow.

As a Christian, this man was unafraid to share his faith and articulate his view of the hereafter. The chaplain's visits were lively, and the care recipient always sought to teach the chaplain in his own way.

He spoke pointedly about a tomorrow of peace, devoid of pain, where the perils of the past will be erased.

As the chaplain looked in the congregation, he could see family members, well-wishers, and friends who were touched by the deceased. And so he shared the following letter about an encounter he had with the care recipient before his death.

Dear Friends,

You hear this letter being read at my funeral because I am no longer with you. I have lived long and hard and have served you with distinction and grace. Yet I lay before you lifeless, a reminder of our frailty. Today, you may say great things about me or seek to praise or denigrate me, but I won't hear. I shall not smell the fragrance of the sweet roses on my casket. I shall not feel your tender touch or bask in our moments of reflection.

However, I want you to know that there is a brighter tomorrow of peace. I look forward to meeting you tomorrow when the flower never fades and the song never dies. I hope to see you tomorrow without pain, poverty, or predicament. I hope to see you in the splendor of my youth. I hope to see you in a place where pain cannot exist in its atmosphere. I shall see you in my great tomorrow when you understand that you were never alone through life's difficult moments. I shall see you in that far off tomorrow where there is no more pain, crying, dying, or separation for the former things are passed away. I shall hear the sounds of hope in that great tomorrow. The majestic symphony of all gathered in that glorious land shall ring through eternity. I shall sing our songs of care and tears all passed forever. As I move with the rhythm of love and dance to the tune of happiness, I pray you will be there, where there is peace forever. Amen.

As the Chaplain recalled that memory, hope whispered, "There is a brighter tomorrow." The perils of this life will not last forever. We can heal. We must heal. May the sounds of hope roll over hills and valleys. May the sounds of hope rise above this world's miasma and declare a brighter tomorrow.

## Your Meditation Moment

Dear God of Hope, Inspire me to hold fast in a broken world. Instruct me in the way I should go. Infuse me with passion and courage to hold fast until you invite me to dwell with you forever. Amen.

## Think and Talk It Through

1. What is your concept of life after death?
2. How do you feel about the future?
3. Write a letter of last words that you would like to be read at your funeral.

# AFTERWORD

LIFE IS DIFFICULT, BUT ALL HOPE IS NOT LOST. ALL of us have experienced mountaintop moments and traversed the valley's vicissitudes. Many of us have walked in the cold dark night of suffering and felt the wind of uncertainty on our faces. We have felt the lash of discouragement and the pangs of pain. We have wandered aimlessly in the dark nights of our existence and the frightening prospects of tomorrow.

But we are not without hope, for the day will break. The light will shine again, and the darkness will be eclipsed by the radiance of the Son who shines on us in a new day. Our past of pain, problems, and pessimism will fade into oblivion. We shall hear again the sounds of hope reverberating through our lived experiences. And when hope personified shall speak, we will hear that we are not alone. We will hear hopeful and joyful tones saying, "Walk on, for I am with you."

The sounds of hope with its marvelous melody shall ring in our hearts. It shall remind us that we are loved, and love trumps hate every time. Its peaceful rhythm shall resonate with those torn apart by wars, fears, and anxieties. Hope's blessed beat shall intensify and fill hearts maligned and misunderstood with joy occupying the empty spaces with singing. And when perplexed by the tragedies of life, hope's sound will beat back the frightening tones of uncertainty. Hope shall be echoed in the dark places of our lives, and every valley of discontent shall hear there is a brighter tomorrow.

Hope will not lose its joyful sound with time but will forever resonate with all who will embrace its melody, beauty, richness of its tones, and surpassing loveliness. The sounds of hope shall be as eternal as the God who gave birth to it.

CPSIA information can be obtained
at www.ICGtesting.com
Printed in the USA
LVHW040710300323
742983LV00010B/29